fabric Picture Books

gwen marston

American Quilter's Society

P. O. Box 3290 • Paducah, KY 42002-3290

www.AQSquilt.com

Located in Paducah, Kentucky, the American Quilter's Society (AQS)
is dedicated to promoting the accomplishments of today's quilters.
Through its publications and events, AQS strives to honor today's
quiltmakers and their work and to inspire future creativity and innovation in quiltmaking.

Editor: Shelley Hawkins
Graphic Design: Lisa M. Clark
Cover Design: Michael Buckingham
Photography: Charles R. Lynch (unless otherwise noted)

Library of Congress Cataloging-in-Publication Data
Marston, Gwen.
     Fabric picture books / by Gwen Marston.
  p. cm.
  ISBN 1-57432-785-2
  1. Textile crafts. 2. Book design. I. Title.
TT699 .M387 2002
746--dc21

2001008087

Additional copies of this book may be ordered from the
American Quilter's Society, PO Box 3290, Paducah, KY 42002-3290,
or online at www.AQSquilt.com.

Dedication

I dedicate this book to Grady Marston,
my first grandchild.

Photo by Brenda Marston.

contents

Fabric from the author's collection

Fabric from the author's collection

introduction

The idea for making fabric picture books developed when I became a grandmother. When my daughter brought my grandson, Grady, home from the hospital, he was wrapped in a quilt made by Grandma Gwenny.

Little Grady immediately worked his magic on me. I had previously made picture quilts similar to the books that would later develop. When the grandbaby came, I was inspired to make this new family member his own picture book collection. The concept of making a personalized library was a breakthrough. Although cloth baby books have been around for a long time, there is nothing quite like these books. The discovery of these calico picture books has been exhilarating for me.

With Grady's mom being a librarian, I couldn't wait to start on the books. In no time at all, 12 Grady Baby books, as I refer to them, were made for my grandson. As I continue to make fabric books for all occasions, these books are a delight to the maker and receiver.

Fabric swatches from top to bottom:
RJR FASHION FABRICS
"Cherry Lane"
Pattern #3939-3

ROBERT KAUFMAN FINE FABRICS
"Crazy for Daisy"
Pattern #AJS2706-3, blue

MARCUS BROTHERS
"Aunt Grace Flannels"
Pattern #T439, color 126D

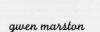
gwen marston

picture book
concepts

Fabric from the
author's collection

Fabric books are perfect for a young child because the pages won't tear and the books last forever. You can make one or two as a gift, or even a whole library for the special baby in your life. Some quilters find it difficult to keep up with the steady flow of new grandbabies when making quilts. These books are quicker and easier to make than a baby quilt because they can be made in one day. Making personalized fabric books for the new arrivals is a lovely sentiment.

Not only are fabric books perfect for babies, they are versatile enough to complement anyone's interests. Everyone I know would love to have a picture book made just for them. What charming birthday and Christmas gifts

gwen marston

Top. *Liberated House and Star*, 5½" x 6½". Designed and made by the author. Star technique by Sandie Dolbee.

Bottom. *Kathy's Chair*, 5½" x 7". Designed and made by Kathy Peters, Marquette, Michigan.

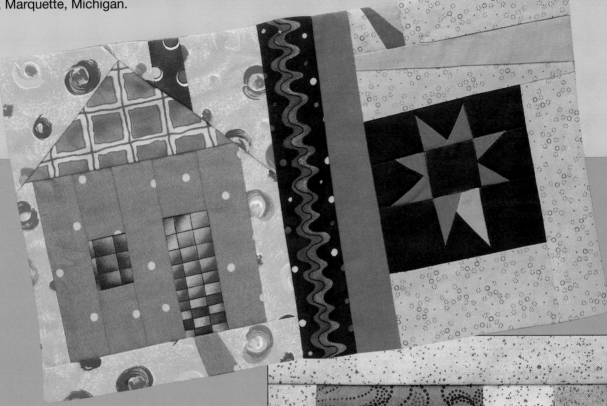

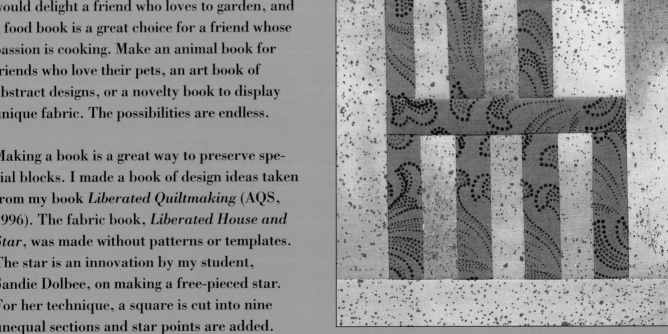

these books make for friends. A garden book would delight a friend who loves to garden, and a food book is a great choice for a friend whose passion is cooking. Make an animal book for friends who love their pets, an art book of abstract designs, or a novelty book to display unique fabric. The possibilities are endless.

Making a book is a great way to preserve special blocks. I made a book of design ideas taken from my book *Liberated Quiltmaking* (AQS, 1996). The fabric book, *Liberated House and Star*, was made without patterns or templates. The star is an innovation by my student, Sandie Dolbee, on making a free-pieced star. For her technique, a square is cut into nine unequal sections and star points are added.

Top. *Re-cut Nine Patch*, 5½" x 7".
Designed and made by the author.

Bottom. *Basket*, 5½" x 7". Designed and
made by the author.

As I travel the country to teach, I notice that quilt-guild presidents are often honored by a gift of a quilt, and more often, a gift of a quilt top. A finished project, such as a book containing guild memories, would be a novel gesture. I have a book of pieced blocks and a book of appliqué patterns, both made and signed by friends. What wonderful books these are to enjoy and share!

Fabric books are fun and easy to make, and they provide an opportunity to showcase your creative abilities. Choose a theme and make a gift for a friend or family member.

Fractured Four Patch, 5½" x 7". Designed and made by the author.

Grady Baby Books

Picture books help a child develop a keen sense of awareness and a lively imagination. They illustrate one of the big differences between radio and television. Hearing a story told over the radio creates visions in your mind far more dramatic and imaginative than television is able to portray. Anyone who remembers gathering around a radio to listen to *The Lone Ranger* or *The Shadow Knows* recalls the excitement these stories generated. These books, without words, provide the opportunity for a mother and child to make up their own stories.

Left. *Grady's Food Book*, 5½" x 6½". Designed and made by the author. Photos by Jay Sailors. I have found a wide variety of stunning fabrics featuring fruits and vegetables. This book includes pictures of eggplant, plums, carrots, blackberries, cabbage, watermelon, cherries, and more. Surrounding these images are equally delectable fabrics. I hope Grady will find these foods irresistible.

Opposite page, left. Grady (top). Photo by Brenda Marston.

South of the Border, 5½" x 6½". Designed and made by the author. This book includes images of festive señoritas on the move, surrounded by maracas, guitars, and chili peppers. Other pages showcase a cactus, sombreros, and mandolins framed in playful prints that remind me of Mexico.

Opposite page, right. *Heavy Equipment*, 5½" x 6½". Designed and made by the author. Photos by Jay Sailors. This book features different prints containing a tractor, road grader, and cement mixer. With rugged machinery that can handle any job, this book will build a constructive imagination.

gwen marston

gwen marston

Novelty fabrics that depict insects, clothing, sports, foods, household items such as dishes, transportation, and children playing are plentiful. My grandson became my experimenter for the appeal fabric picture books have with babies. Grady loved these books from the time he was able to pick them up on his own. At that stage, he could grab them, throw them around, and best of all, put them in his mouth. Soon after that, he was looking at the pictures, turning the pages, and pointing at the images.

One of Grady's favorite books is *Friendly Faces*. As he sits on his mom's lap, she turns the pages and says, "Here is a baby with red hair, and here is a baby with black hair, and here is a baby with three hairs." From an early age, Grady is realizing the joys that books hold.

As a great medium for self expression, each book carries a special message from the maker. When making Grady's books, I considered subjects I wanted him to know about. The

Friendly Faces, 5½" x 6½". Designed and made by the author. This book portrays playmates from the neighborhood. There are nine portraits of adorable kids, framed in fabrics just as playful. Babies enjoy looking at faces, so I am confident your baby will love turning these pages.

gwen marston

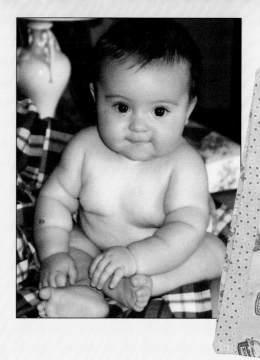

thing my daughter loves about these books is that her baby can enjoy his grandma's artwork from an early age.

The following books comprise Grady's first library, which is continually expanding: *The Farm*, *Wild Animals*, *The Great Southwest*, *Heavy Equipment*, *Gardening*, *Friendly Faces*, *Alphabet Soup*, *Foods*, *South of the Border*, *Just Makin' Conversation*, and *Elvis Presley*. Grady also has a book of common pieced quilt patterns so he can recognize the difference between a Nine-Patch and a Shoofly when he sees them, as he surely will.

Becoming a grandmother was a much grander event than I'd imagined. In this world of increased mobility, I don't see my grandchild as often as preferred. These books help me send specific messages to Grady in concrete form. Once confident that Grady had enough reading material for his first year, I began thinking about other people who would enjoy these little creations.

Above. *Just Makin' Conversation*, 5½" x 6½". Designed and made by the author. Made with 1930s reproduction fabrics. Bunnies, clowns, scissors, and spools of thread surround images of children playing together. These images are sure to spark a child's curiosity.

Top left. Grady sitting on his mama's lap. Photo by Sarah Simpkins.

Opposite page, top. *Gwen's Appliqué Book*, 5½" x 6½". Designed and made by the author. Made from cheater cloth.

Opposite page, bottom. *Dandelion*, 6" x 8". Designed and made by Ellen Heck, Somis, California. Ellen and I became friends when we taught together in California. Specializing in botanically correct original appliqué, Ellen designed the Centennial Quilt for her home state.

Remembering Piercy: 1983–2000, 5½" x 7". Designed and made by the author. For the Pierson memory book, beautiful soft pastels were chosen to reflect his sweet, gentle spirit. Floral prints were appropriate because Pierson always enjoyed laying in my flowers. For more about Pierson, see Resources, page 46.

Photo Transfer Books

You can make family photo albums that will be cherished for a lifetime with photo transfer techniques. The following are a few ideas:

- A book for the new baby in your family that shows pictures of grandparents, aunts, and uncles. Because relatives do not always live close by, this is a good way for a baby to become familiar with the family.
- A memory book with pictures of baby's first year for a special child in your life.
- A wedding anniversary book for your parents.
- A memory book to honor a special pet.

I enjoyed the company of my dog, Pierson, for 17 years. Three weeks after his death, my grandson came into the world. These two events remind me of how life replenishes itself. It's good to remember that sorrow will eventually be followed by joy. Making a memory book for Piercy and making baby books for Grady helped me both grieve and rejoice in these two major events in my life.

Appliqué Books

Make a book of floral appliqués for a friend who loves to garden or appliqué. I asked some of my friends to make a page for me to compile in a book. My appliqué book is not only the most beautiful book in my collection, it was the fastest to make. It's amazing how fast a book can go together when your friends make all the pages.

When asking friends to contribute pages to your book, here are some guidelines for instructions:

- The appliqué design should not exceed 5" x 6½".
- Give the exact size you want the background to be. Ask that the background be cut slightly larger than the exact size, and explain that you will size the blocks to 5½" x 7".
- Ask your friends to sign their pages.

My appliqué book is a collection of original designs by quilters I consider to be at the top of their class. Best of all, these pages were made

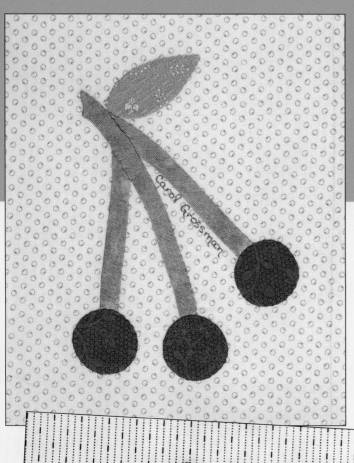

Top. *Cherries*, 6" x 8". Designed and made by Carol Grossman, Rochester Hills, Michigan. Carol was inspired by the fall colors of the cherry trees in her backyard. When designing this motif, she clipped some branches, then matched the colors.

Bottom. *Bird with Tulip*, 6" x 8". Designed and made by Erena Rieflin, Rochester Hills, Michigan. Erena is one of the best technicians I know. Nobody's better at putting it together than Erena.

by really great women who I'm privileged to count as friends. Knowing them has enriched my life in many ways. This book reminds me of the importance of friendship.

An easier way still to make a book of appliqué blocks is to buy pre-printed fabric. I found fabric with 19 stunning appliqué patterns and made a book (page 15). In keeping with the nineteenth-century appliqué designs, I used reproduction prints to frame each block. These images don't require complicated piecing because a simple frame makes a beautiful accent.

Opposite page, top. *Grady's Bird Identification Book*, 5½" x 6½". Designed and made by the author. An abstract butterfly print is the dominant fabric in this book. Print from the bird fabric's selvage was chosen for the title of this book (see Salvaging Selvages, page 32).

Opposite page, bottom. *Black-Capped Chickadee*, 3" x 3". The chickadee was designed and made by Margaret Rolfe. I created a bird-in-the-garden effect by surrounding the chickadee with a floral and bird print on a sky blue background.

Special-Interest Books

BIRD BOOKS

If you are a bird watcher or know someone who loves birds, a bird book is sure to please. This chickadee was given to me by Margaret Rolfe. Margaret is a quilt historian, author, and quiltmaker from Australia. She is known for her life-like bird and animal designs. The patterns from her book, *Go Wild with Quilts* (That Patchwork Place, 1993), are perfect for making pages in a bird identification book.

If you don't have time to piece the birds for your book, you can find fabric printed with birds. I made a field identification book for my grandson. Beginning with such lovely images, I wanted to frame the birds in equally lovely fabrics. Several different fabrics are typically used in my books; however, this book has a limited number of support fabrics.

FISHING BOOKS

A fishing book would make a splash with the fisherman in your family. For someone who has only caught one small fish in her life, I was rather surprised by the amount of fish fabric in my cupboard. I found beautiful fish, flys, fishing poles, and reels, as well as fishing advice on the fabric. For example, "Small mouth bass found in lakes and rivers" and "Summer is the time for the stealthy pursuit of sea trout by night." Who would have known?

Fishing Book, 5½" x 6½". Designed and made by the author.

PRETEEN BOOKS

I asked a friend of mine with a preteen child what children that age are into these days. She gave me a long list of things that would appeal to these energetic kids. I made a book reflecting some of these interests, including computer games, sports, scooters, skateboards, Monopoly, fast foods, spiked and colored hair, guitars, coffee, and dinosaurs. Preteens also like bright colors and wild prints. Finding fabrics that match the interests of someone special in your life is fun and often easy with the wide assortment of novelty fabrics available.

Preteen Book, 5½" x 6½". Designed and made by the author.

Alphabet Soup Books

In the beginning, my preference was to develop each book around a theme. Now I enjoy making books with an interesting mix of unrelated images, which I call Alphabet Soup books.

When making these books, I think it's effective if each page is surprisingly different. For a child, an unanticipated image on every page can be captivating. Panda bears, bananas, airplanes, shoes, chickens, pies and cakes, frogs, and of course, Elvis, can be combined to make a one-of-a-kind book. Alphabet Soup books can include just about anything. They provide an opportunity to explore a wide variety of fabrics.

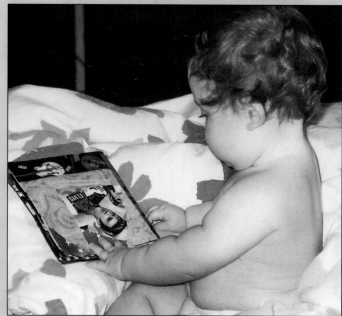

Top. *Timeless Treasures*, 5½" x 6½". Designed and made by the author.

Bottom. Grady admiring a picture of Elvis. Photo by Brenda Marston.

Timeless Treasures [cover], 5½" x 6½". Designed and made by the author.

Above. *Alphabet Soup*, 5½" x 6½".
Designed and made by the author.

Below. *Girl with Cat*, 5½" x 6½".
Designed and made by the author.

picture book basics

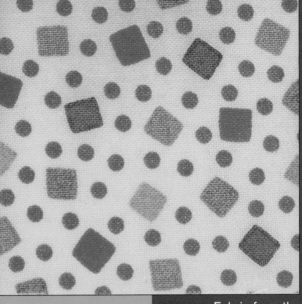

Fabric from the
author's collection

When designing fabric picture books, consider the type of book you are making as well as the recipient. Both theme books, in which a specific theme is developed, and Alphabet Soup books, in which a mix of wonderful images is presented, are suitable for children or adults.

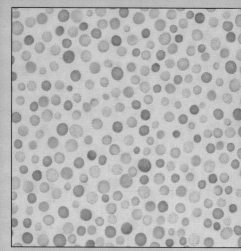

ROBERT KAUFMAN FINE FABRICS
"Crazy for Daisy"
Pattern #AJS2705-8, white

SOUTH SEA IMPORTS
KidStuff™ "Once Upon a Time"
Pattern #31285, color 634

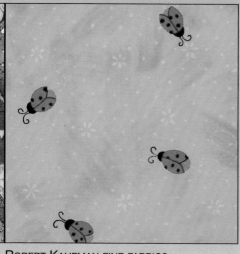

ROBERT KAUFMAN FINE FABRICS
In the Nursery "Lady Bug"
Pattern #AJS-2873-3, green

FABRIC TRADITIONS
"Major League Baseball®"
Pattern #7429-B

ROBERT KAUFMAN FINE FABRICS
"The Birds & The Bees"
Pattern #AJB-2937-2, canary

Choosing Fabric

With so many character prints available, it is easy to find fabric for books. Perhaps the production of these prints has increased as a result of the interest in making "I Spy" quilts, although I don't know which came first. "I Spy" quilts are a fabric response to the popular childhood game. Because of their current popularity, there is an amazing array of captivating prints that is sure to cover any topic you choose.

These books gave me a good excuse to buy a lot of new fabric. Because it doesn't take much fabric to make a little book, I can buy a bit of everything I like. Fat quarters go far when making small pieces. There are endless fabric combinations. In choosing fabric, the

PETER PAN FABRICS
"American Kennel"
Pattern #1304, color 47

MARCUS BROTHERS
"Aunt Grace Flannels"
Pattern #T438, 120D

FABRI-QUILT
"Neon Forest"
Pattern #74601, jungle animals

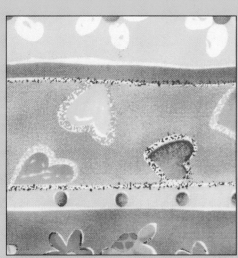

ROBERT KAUFMAN FINE FABRICS
"Crazy for Daisy"
Pattern #AJS2707-4, bright

key is to find fabrics that complement each
other to make a gorgeous book.

Designers have made finding complementary
fabrics easy. In many cases, specific fabric
lines are designed to go together. For example,
1930s reproduction fabrics naturally go
together. I used these prints in *Just Makin'
Conversation* (page 13).

When making the Grady Baby books, I
deliberately chose fabrics that would catch a
baby's eye. I was attracted to the wonderful
bright colors that are currently on the market.
The fabrics with polka dots and wiggly lines
are my personal favorites. Using fabrics that
you are comfortable with increases the chances
that you will be happy with the results.

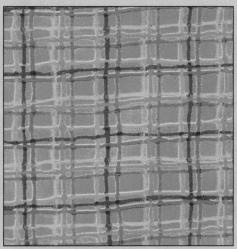

SOUTH SEA IMPORTS
KidStuff™ "Once Upon a Time"
Pattern #3129, color 436

Combining fabrics that support each other makes the completed image stronger. Consider the following examples. A chicken surrounded by feather fabric or a paint can and brush combined with crayons are obvious combinations that work well together.

Above. *Christmas*, 5½" x 7". Designed and made by the author.
With the marvelous Christmas fabric available, it would be easy to tell a Christmas story in fabric. In fact, nearly every holiday is represented in fabric. You can delight friends and family with special books to help celebrate the holidays. Christmas prints with festive scenes require only a simple-pieced frame. With the holiday season being such a busy time, fabric books are ideal to make as gifts.

Below. *Bunnies*, 5½" x 7". Designed and made by the author. The fabrics you choose help tell the story. I used delicate pastels to say, "It's Easter," in the book *Bunnies*.

Organizing Fabric

When I began making fabric books, there were so many little pieces of new fabric that it was difficult to keep track of them. Each time a new book was made, I would scatter all my fabric on the floor and sort through every piece trying to find the appropriate fabric. This was pretty frustrating, so I devised a solution. I organized the fabric by subject matter and sorted it in plastic bags. The gallon-size bags work best for me. With each bag labeled, finding the fabric I need takes no time at all.

Design and Color

Both complex and simple piecing work when designing a composition. In the following examples, the complexity of the piecing coupled with the use of more prints adds to the energetic quality of the *Girl with Pigtails*. The simple piecing works well around the *Girl in Green*.

In both cases, fabrics that echo the playful nature of the central images were used. Furthermore, the dominant colors in the images were repeated, although this is not a prerequisite for good design. As you design, think in terms of making each page a complete composition.

Above. *Girl in Green*, 5½" x 7". Example of simple piecing.

Opposite page. *Girl with Pigtails*, 5½" x 7". Example of complex piecing.

Salvaging Selvages

Never underestimate the uses for selvage. Over the years, I've learned that there are as many uses for it as there are for duct tape. I use selvage to wrap gifts, pull my hair back when I'm sewing, and tie tomato plants. I have been saving words on selvage for years and have an interesting collection. The word "Tools," printed on the selvage of fabric, made the perfect title for a book full of screwdrivers, drills, nuts, and bolts.

Here is a short list of selvages I've collected as possible book titles: *Galaxy Garden, Crafted with Pride in the U.S.A., Barnyard Buddies, Possibilities, Bunny Bumpkins, Sweeties, Sunday In The Park, Lollipops, Hedgehog, Galaxy Garden, Nine Lives and Old Wives, In the Beginning, Rainbow Critters,*

Go! With Dick and Jane, 5½" x 7".
Designed and made by the author.

Figure 1a. Sew the very edge of the selvage to another fabric piece, leaving a ¼" seam allowance on the fabric piece.

Figure 1b. Press the seam allowance toward the fabric piece.

Figure 2. Top stitch the edge of the selvage if the word is too close to the edge to piece.

Material Pleasures, Chickens, Playtime, Kid Stuff, and *Matters of the Heart.*

Occasionally, the perfect title for your book can be found on words printed on the fabric. Most often, the words appear on the very edge of the selvage, making a ¼" seam allowance impossible without loosing the word. However, there is an easy way to join it to a raw edge. Move the selvage slightly away from the fabric edge, so as you stitch ¼" on the raw edge, you are barely on the edge of the selvage (Figure 1). Since the selvage is not a raw edge, the normal seam allowance is not necessary.

Another way to handle selvage where the word is too close to the edge is to simply top stitch the edge (Figure 2).

Left. *Haiku Cat*, 5½" x 7". Designed and made by the author.

Bottom. *Tools*, 5½" x 7". Designed and made by the author. Often, just the right words for a title appear on the selvage of character prints.

gwen marston

picture book
construction

Fabric from the
author's collection

Constructing a book is as easy as cutting out
the featured picture, adding pieces of fabric,
pressing, and trimming as you work. Designs
that look complicated are easy to construct.
The general rule is if something is too small,
add on, and if it is too large, trim. Pages can
be made with pre-cut strips or scraps of fabric.

Fabric swatch below:
SOUTH SEA IMPORTS
KidStuff™ "Once Upon a Time"
Pattern #31287, color 473

Opposite page, left:
Left. ROBERT KAUFMAN FINE FABRICS
"The Birds & The Bees"
Pattern #AJB-2939-4, strawberry

Right. Fabric from the author's
collection

Pear, 5½" x 7". Designed and made by the author.

Making Pages with Strips

In this method of page construction, begin by cutting several strips the width you desire for your design. Interesting angles can be created by simply sewing on a straight strip and then cutting it crooked.

When cutting strips, use a rotary cutter and a quilter's ruler to straighten the edge each time you add an irregular piece. These tools make a quick cut and a straight edge. For best results, press after every addition and before you trim.

gwen marston

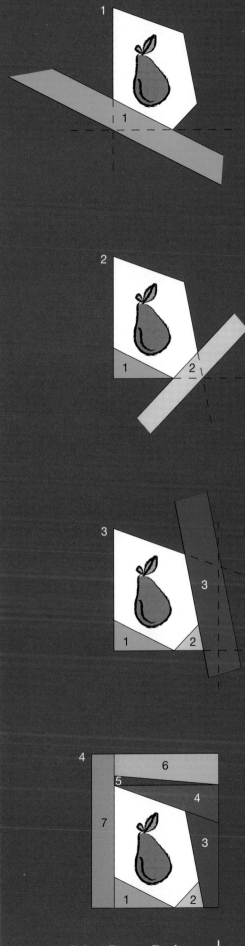

Figure 3. Add strips to the center image, press and trim, and add additional strips.

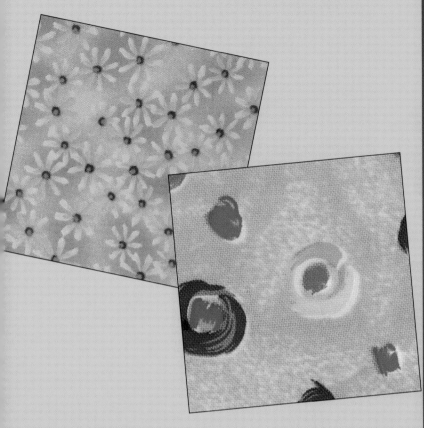

PAGE CONSTRUCTION

1. Cut out the center image and sew on a strip of fabric.
2. Press and trim as shown by the dotted lines.
3. Continue adding strips in this manner until the page is complete (see Figure 3, steps 1–4).

When working with strips, there are usually several leftover pieces that can come in handy later. After making many books, I have quite a collection of scraps. When I begin work on another book, I have a good variety of fabrics pre-cut, organized, and ready to use. Little fabric goes to waste at my house.

gwen marston

Figure 4. Adding scraps to odd-shaped pieces so they can be joined.

Making Pages with Scraps

Joining odd-sized shapes is a matter of determining where fabric needs to be added to create a straight seam. To join the images on the black fabric in the following example (Figure 4), I added pieces of fabric to all three shapes, pressed, and straightened the edges so the three units could be joined. To ensure the three sections would be large enough to fit together, I sewed oversized scraps to the black shapes. Once these three units are joined, other pieces need to be added until the unit is large enough to square to size. Once again, add on or trim to achieve the desired size.

For determining the angle of a triangle needed to square up an odd-sized image, lay the image in the corner of the fabric to be added, right sides up, and cut along the edge of the image (Figure 5).

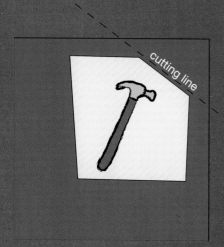

cutting line

Figure 5. Marking the angle needed to square an odd-sized image.

Pressing and Squaring Pages

In most cases, press the seam allowances to the outside, as you would if you were making a Log Cabin block by conventional construction methods. However, if the seam allowances naturally want to lie in another direction, my advice is not to argue with them.

Make the pages slightly larger than needed. Spray with starch and square to size. It is important to be accurate in sizing the pages. Proper pressing, stabilizing the pages with starch, and careful measuring are the secrets of achieving a professional-looking page.

A good size for picture books is between 3½" x 4" and 8" x 9½". Certainly, there comes a point when a book becomes too large, and it might as well be called a quilt. With a few exceptions, I have been consistent in the size of my books.

I wanted the Grady Baby books to be the same size so they would look like a little library when lined up on Grady's bookshelf. The finished size of these books is 5½" x 6½". I squared the pages to 5½" x 7". With the addition of the 1½" spine, which adds the exact same width lost by the seam allowance, the finished size is 5½" x 6½".

I also made a delightful set of little books. These tiny books measure just over 3". They have proved to be so enchanting, they instantly bring a smile to the face of the reader. When making these tiny books,

Fabric swatches
from top to bottom:
FABRIC TRADITIONS
"Rodeo"
Pattern #4838-A

ROBERT KAUFMAN
FINE FABRICS
In the Nursery
"Cotton Balls"
Pattern #AJS-2877-4,
melon

MARCUS BROTHERS
"Olé"
Pattern #G151-111w

SOUTH SEA IMPORTS
KidStuff™
"Once Upon a Time"
Pattern #31286,
color 586

Fabric from the
author's collection

Examples of 3" books.

I squared the pages to 3" x 3½". The spine was cut to 1½" x 3½". Of course, these measurements can be altered in any number of ways. Squaring the pages to 3½" x 4½" results in a slightly rectangular book measuring 3½" x 4" when finished. Even this small book size can accommodate either eight or twelve pages with ease.

Grady enjoying one of his fabric picture books.
Photo by Brenda Marston.

Book Assembly

Books can have either eight or twelve pages.
Any more than that will make the book too
difficult to sew. The pages are made into units
similar to the method of making a pillow slip.

MAKING PAGE UNITS

1. Cut spines 1½" x 7" (or the length of the
    page). You will need four spines for an
    eight-page book and six spines for a
    twelve-page book.

2. Arrange the pages right side up in pairs
    as shown in Figure 6. Sew a spine
    between each pair, as shown in Figure 7
    on the following page. Press seam
    allowances toward the spine. Spray the
    pairs on the right sides with heavy starch
    and press again.

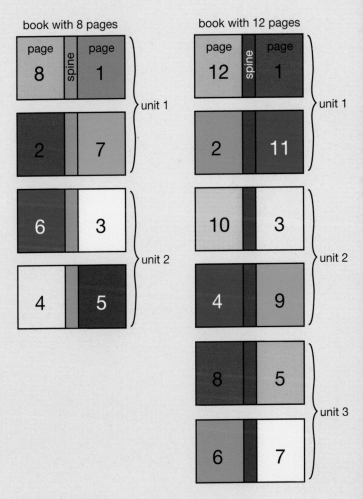

Figure 6. Page layout charts.

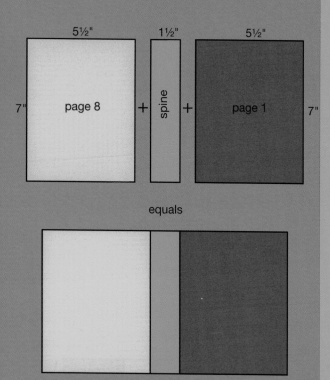

5½"　　1½"　　5½"

7"　page 8　+　spine　+　page 1　7"

equals

Figure 7. Join the pages with the spine.

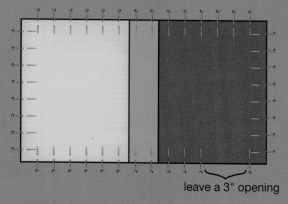

leave a 3" opening

Figure 8. Pin the pages every 1½".

3. Whether you are making an eight-page or twelve-page book, place the first and second pairs of pages right sides together to form the first unit. Align the seams for the spines and pin the pages together along their edges every 1½" (Figure 8).

4. Start on the bottom edge (Figure 9, page 43), sew one side of the pair together with a ¼" seam allowance. At the end of the seam, sew off the edge, lift the presser foot, turn the pages a quarter turn and, starting at the edge again, sew the next side. Sew all four sides this way, leaving a 3" opening on the bottom edge. (For easier sewing, try to leave the opening where there are no pieced seams.)

5. To turn the piece right side out, fold one side's seam allowances down and fold the adjacent side's allowances over the first (Figure 10, page 43). Holding the folded corner with one hand, slip your other hand inside and grab the folded corner with finger and thumb. Pull the corner to the inside. Repeat for all four corners, then turn the entire unit right side out. Press.

6. Use a thread that matches the top page to sew the opening closed with a blind stitch. (To keep the thread from showing on the back page, which may not match the color, slip the needle through the fold on the back page and bring it up through the top page.) Spray starch and press the unit again.

7. For the second unit, place the pairs right sides together, align the spine seams, and pin as before. Trim ¹⁄₁₆" off of both sides of the pages, but not the top and bottom. You need to trim because the accumulation of folds is likely to make the center units extend beyond the outer cover unit. Follow steps 4–6 to finish the second unit.

8. If your book has a third unit, trim the sides of this unit slightly more than ¹⁄₁₆" to keep the pages even with each other. Finish the third unit as you did the other two.

JOINING PAGE UNITS

9. Arrange the units in order. Align the spine seams and secure with a few pins. Place the pinned units with the outside cover facing up. Mark the center of the spine by laying a ruler down the middle of the spine and either drawing a pencil line or scratching a line with a pin.

10. To sew the units together, use a thread that matches the spine. Begin with three or four back stitches and slowly sew down the pencil line on the spine (Figure 11). Without clipping the threads at the end of the seam, turn the book around and sew a second line of stitching, ending with a few back stitches. (The second line can be stitched on top of the first one or about ¹⁄₁₆" from the first line. Both methods work well.)

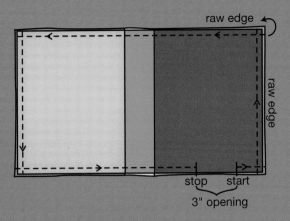

Figure 9. Sew off the edge of each side, leaving a 3" opening at the bottom.

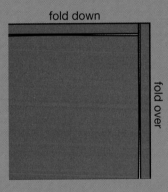

Figure 10. Turn the adjacent corner over the first corner.

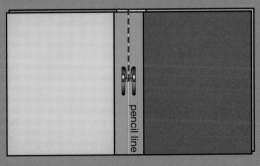

Figure 11. Sew down the pencil line on the spine to join the units.

Polka dot fabric
from the author's
collection

gwen marston

picture book
conclusion

Fabric from the
author's collection

Good things come in small packages. My
grandson was my inspiration for developing
fabric picture books. Through the joy he and
others receive from these charming books, I
have been inspired to continue making these
fabric picture books.

I hope you have fun creating your own
one-of-a-kind fabric picture books. The
construction methods ensure that your book
will be so original, you won't even be able to
copy yourself. Enjoy!

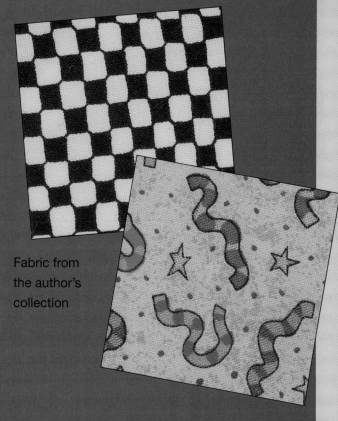

Fabric from the author's collection

Other Books by the Author

American Beauties: Rose and Tulip Quilts, AQS, 1988.

Amish Quilting Patterns, Dover Publications, Inc. 1987.

Liberated Quiltmaking, AQS, 1996.

Mary Schafer and Her Quilts, Michigan State University Press, 1990.

Q is For Quilt, Michigan State University Press, 1987.

Quilting with Style, Principles for Great Pattern Design, AQS, 1993.

Sets and Borders, AQS, 1987.

Twenty Little Amish Quilts, Dover Publications, Inc., 1993.

Twenty Little Four Patch Quilts, Dover Publications, Inc., 1996.

Twenty Little Log Cabin Quilts, Dover Publications, Inc., 1995.

Twenty Little Patchwork Quilts, Dover Publications, Inc., 1990.

Twenty Little Pinwheel Quilts, Dover Publications, Inc., 1994.

Twenty Little Triangle Quilts, Dover Publications, Inc., 1997.

70 Classic Quilting Patterns, Dover Publications, Inc., 1987.

Resources

Go Wild with Quilts, Margaret Rolfe, That Patchwork Place, Inc., Bothell, WA, 1993.

Go Wild with Quilts – Again!, Margaret Rolfe, That Patchwork Place, Inc., Bothell, WA, 1995.

Liberated Quiltmaking, Gwen Marston, AQS, Paducah, KY, 1996.

The Signature Quilt: Traditions, Techniques and The Signature Block Collection, Pepper Cory and Susan McKelvey, Quilt House Publishing, Saddle Brook, NJ, 1995.

For more about Pierson, see *Through the Garden Gate*, Jean and Valori Wells, C&T Publishing, Inc., Lafayette, CA, 1999, page 46.

About the Author

Helping quilters realize their own creative abilities, Gwen Marston teaches quiltmaking in the United States as well as Japan. She has enjoyed more than 26 solo exhibits of her work in both of these countries, including seven museum exhibits of her small quilts. Gwen has been a regular columnist for *Lady's Circle Patchwork Quilts* and has authored 15 books, five for AQS. For nearly 20 years, Gwen has hosted annual quilt retreats in her Beaver Island home on Lake Michigan.

Fabric from the author's collection

Self Portrait, 11½" x 13½". Designed and made by the author.

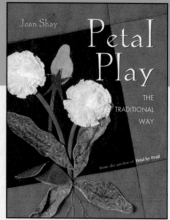

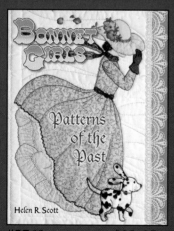

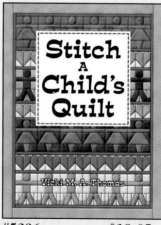